MY BOOK ABOUT THE MASS

NAME charlottevictoria Place ....

ANTHONY BULLEN

My Book about the Mass

ILLUSTRATED BY

MARTIN COOKE

St Paul Publications

St Paul Publications
Middlegreen, Slough SL3 6BT, England

Printed by Chiltern Printers, Slough
ISBN 085439 249 1

St Paul Publications is an activity of the priests and brothers of the Society of St Paul who proclaim the Gospel through the media of social communication.

For Anh Thu and Bao

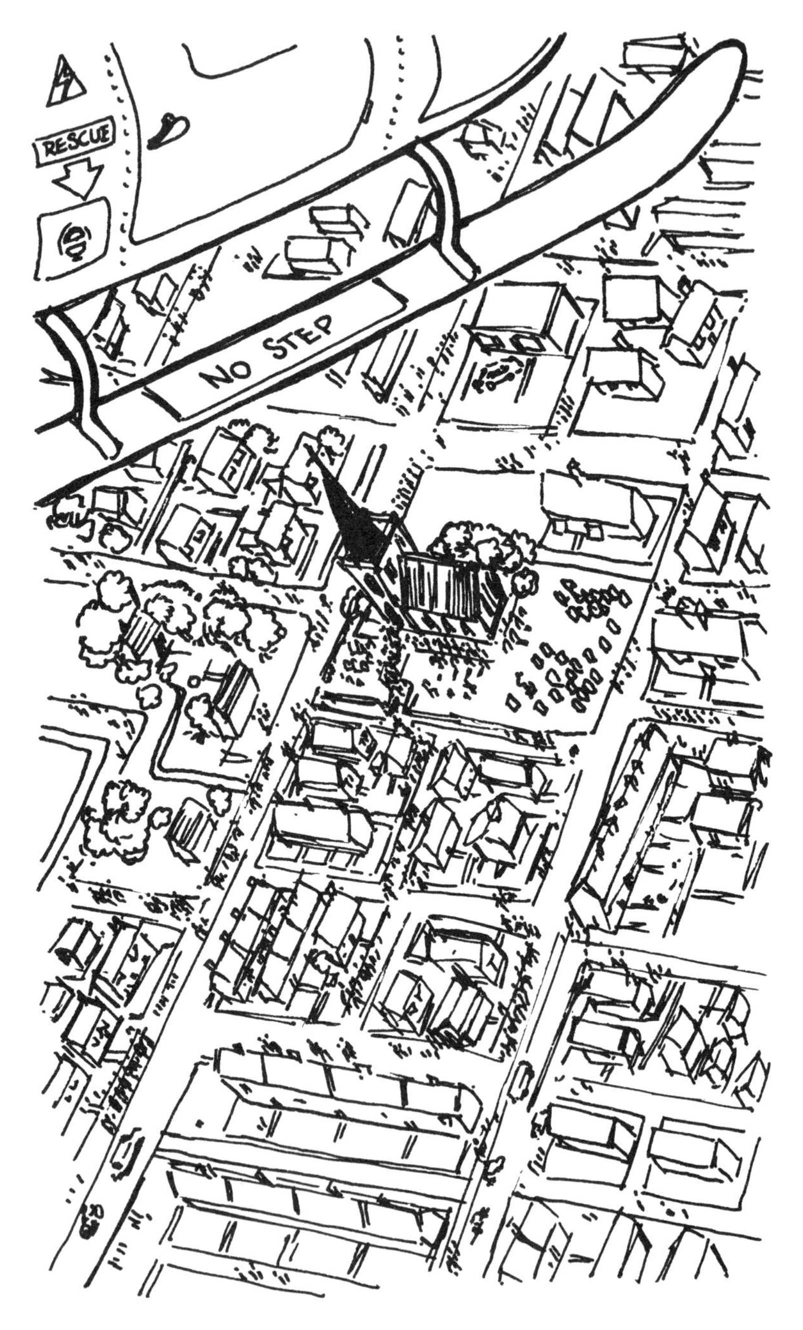
RESCUE
NO STEP

WHEN I WAS NINE

This book is written to help you when you come to Mass.* When I was nine years old, I used to go to Mass with my mother and father. Most often with my mum on weekdays – as my dad had to go out to work. Sometimes I would get very bored and, instead of praying, I would count how many candles were lit in front of Our Lady's statue, or I would close my eyes and daydream. It was only later on when I was older and I found out more about the Mass that I began to enjoy coming. I realise now that the Mass is about

BEING SORRY
LISTENING
CARING
THANKING
MAKING PEACE
GIVING
TALKING
CELEBRATING

and over the next few pages of this little book we will discover together more about each of those eight things.

My mum and dad have both gone to heaven. They loved the Mass so much that they passed that love on to me. And now I would like to pass it on to you.

*Another word for Mass is 'Eucharist'. When we speak of 'Communion', we are talking of that part of the Mass when people receive the white consecrated host (and sometimes the chalice).

GKF
123K

I'M SORRY DAD

The Browns had an old car. They called it the 'Brown Banger'. Young Jimmy loved cars and would like to have driven it but, of course, he was too young.

One day, when his dad was out, he got into the driving seat and pretended to drive. "I wonder what will happen if I let the brake off", he said to himself. He soon found out. The car began to roll slowly backwards into the street. Across the street it went, and banged right into the wall of the house opposite. Jimmy was frightened but not hurt.

What did Mr Brown say when he got home? I'll leave you to guess. And what did Jimmy say? "Dad, I'm very sorry. I was stupid, I won't do anything like that again."

15

I'LL HAVE TO TELL HER

Hannah was in second year Juniors. Her best friend was Helen who had red hair and wore glasses. Hannah doesn't know why she did it but one day when some of the class were making fun of Helen and calling her 'Red Top' and 'Four-eyes', Hannah joined in too. This was too much for Helen and she began to cry. That night when Hannah got home, her mother noticed she was upset. "I've hurt Helen," she said. "And I'll have to tell her I'm sorry." "It's too late now to go to Helen's house," her mother said. "Why not write her a note and your father will take it round to Helen's house later."

And that's what Hannah did.

What do you think she wrote?

BEING SORRY

When the priest comes to the altar at the beginning of the Mass, he asks us to think quietly for a moment of ways in which we may have done wrong. In these quiet moments I try to look back over the week and see how I have behaved:

AT HOME

AT SCHOOL

AT PLAY

I ask myself too how I have been with God my Father: Have I talked with Him and listened to Him? How I have been with Jesus, my Friend and Brother? Have I tried to do the sort of things He would want me to do?

Then in the same sort of way that Jimmy said he was sorry to his father for being so stupid, and Hannah said sorry to Helen for being so mean, I tell God I am sorry.

The key words in this part of the Mass are:

LORD, HAVE MERCY

DO YOU HEAR ME?

Jimmy loved planes. He lived not far from an airport and so knew the makes of many of the aircraft that took off and landed all day long: 747s, DC10s, Tri-stars, even Concordes – he had seen them all. At Christmas his dad had brought him a tiny radio that was specially made for picking up air-to-ground and ground-to-air conversations. Sometimes at night in bed he would switch on and hear this sort of thing:

Captain:	This is Alpha Tango Orange, from Los Angeles calling Heathrow. Can you direct me please.
Ground Control:	Alpha Tango Orange, descend to 9000 at 400 mph. Keep on your present course.
Captain:	Thank you, sir. Can you give me details of wind speed and air temperatures and cloud cover.
Ground Control:	Here are the details you request.

Jimmy realised that if the captain had tried to get the plane into Heathrow without listening to all the information given him by the air-traffic controllers, he might never have landed the plane safely.

WE SIT AND LISTEN

At Mass, one of the readers goes on to the lectern (that is the small desk with the Bible on it). He often reads two passages from God's book, the Bible. The first will often be from that part of the Book that was written before Jesus was born. Then he starts reading a psalm which we join in saying. Jesus said these psalms as His prayers. Next he reads from one of the letters written by the friends of Jesus after He had risen from the dead.

We try very hard to listen and understand because, just like the captain of a plane listens to the directions as to how he is to bring the plane home safely, we listen to God speaking to us through the Bible. He is telling us how we can make the journey safely back to Him, to His home in heaven.

The key words in this part of the Mass are:

THIS IS THE WORD OF THE LORD
THANKS BE TO GOD

Good
News
From
Matthew
Good
News
From
Mark
Good
News
From
Luke
Good
News
From
John

WE STAND FOR JESUS

The priest now comes to the lectern and he is going to read from one of the Gospels. There are four Gospels: Matthew's, Mark's, Luke's, and John's. Each of them contains the words that Jesus said. He speaks to us today through the Gospels. We can hear His voice when the Gospels are read.

Just as we stand for the National Anthem, so when the Gospel is read, we stand up out of respect for Jesus's words.

We make three crosses with the back of our thumb; one on our forehead, one on our lips, one on our heart.

May the words of Jesus be in my mind, on my lips, in my heart.

The key words in this part of the Mass are:

PRAISE TO YOU, LORD JESUS CHRIST

ALL THROUGH THE NIGHT

Not long after Hannah went to bed she began to get toothache. It got worse and worse and she couldn't sleep. In the end she got up and went downstairs. Her mother was doing the ironing. "Mum, I have awful toothache," she said.

Her mother went into the kitchen and made some creamy cocoa, and gave Hannah an aspirin to take with it. Then she took her back to bed and lay down by her side. As she began to doze off, Hannah thought — "How lucky I am to have such a good mum and dad! They care for me all day long."

Next day she went to the dentist and his treatment soon put the matter right. On the way home she thought — "Do I care for other people the way mum and dad care for me?"

THOUSANDS DIE IN EARTHQUAKE!

TRAIN CRASH IN MIDLANDS!

O.A.P. MUGGED

BOAT OVERTURNS – SIX DROWN!

RISE IN JOBLESS FIGURES

DEATH IN GOLD MINE!

MANCHESTER AIR DISASTER

STARVATION IN SUDAN!

LEUKAEMIA WARD FULL!

CRUELTY TO SIX YEAR OLD

FIGHTING IN NORTHERN IRELAND

HAVING A CARE FOR OTHERS

We have a chance to show we care for others at Mass. After the Gospel has been read and the priest has spoken about the words of Jesus, he invites us to pray for other people and their needs. We often pray for people who are starving, for people who are suffering, who haven't got a job and yet they have a family to support, for people involved in hijacks, muggings, volcanoes and earthquakes. These prayers show that we really care for other people. Of course, we try to do more than just pray. Often we will have an opportunity to do without some luxury ourselves and give the money to people who are in need.

The key words for this part of the Mass are:

LORD, HEAR US
LORD, GRACIOUSLY HEAR US

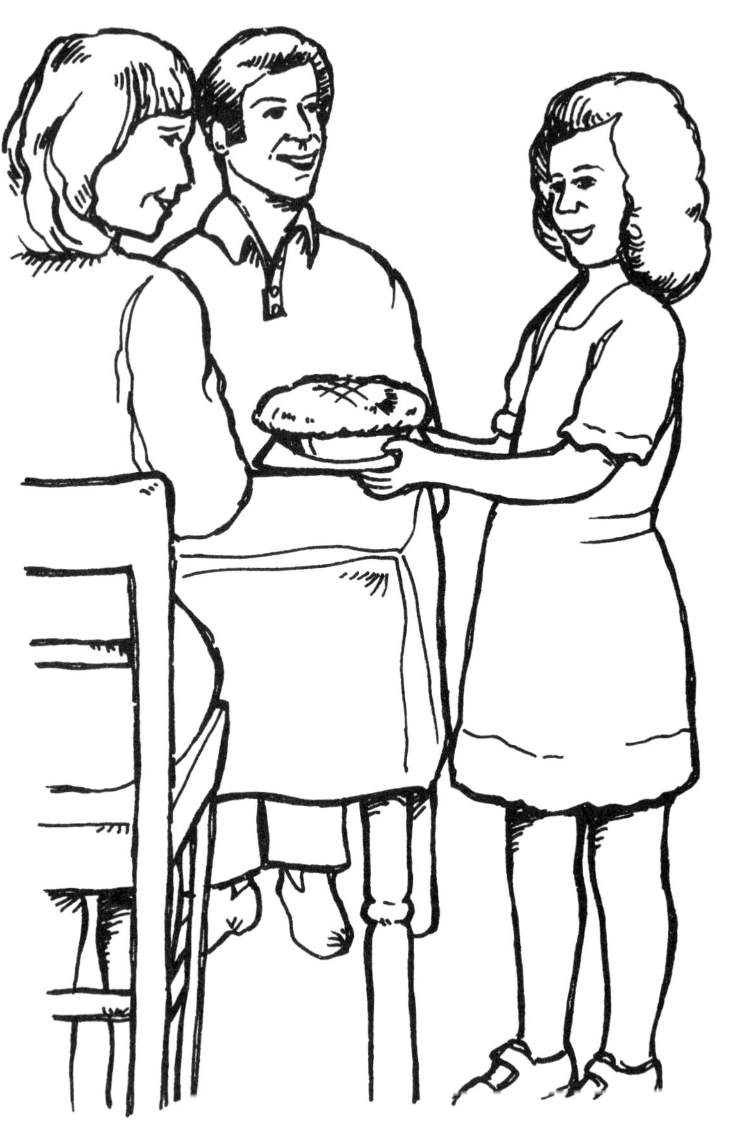

ANNIVERSARY DAY

Hannah overheard her mother on the phone. She was talking to Grandma. "We would like you to come for a meal next Wednesday," she said. "Brian and I will have been married fifteen years: it's our anniversary."

Hannah was quite excited at the idea of a special meal to celebrate her parents' wedding anniversary, and she wondered if she could prepare something special for the occasion.

When she told Helen, her best friend, Helen said, "Why don't you come to our house the day before, and my mum would help you make a nice apple and plum pie." And that's what she did. She managed to get it home and into the bedroom without anyone noticing.

When the celebration meal had started, Hannah said, "I have a surprise." She went upstairs and brought down the pie she had prepared on the special silver dish Helen's mum had lent her.

She walked slowly to the dining table with it. A big smile on her face.

Her parents were very happy at what she had done.

PREPARING THE GIFTS*

The ushers at St Mark's used to ask people as they came into church if they would take the gifts of bread and wine to the altar. Jimmy and his dad one day were asked and they took the wine and one of the containers (called a 'ciborium') holding the small white discs of bread. Hannah took one as well. Behind her walked the ushers who had been collecting money from the people. This money was needed to pay for the lighting and heating of the church and the parish house where the priest lived. It also paid the priest's grocery bills, and the salary he paid the housekeeper.

As Hannah walked forward she thought – "This reminds me of bringing in the present I had prepared for my mum and dad's anniversary."

The key words in this part of the Mass are:

BLESSED BE GOD FOR EVER

*This part of the Mass used to be called 'The Offertory'.

WHERE ARE THE NINE?

"Unclean. We're unclean. Keep away from us," the ten men wailed in their misery. They had a terrible skin disease which could be passed on to others very easily.

But Jesus wasn't afraid of disease. He called them to him and spoke to them. As they were walking away, they noticed that the skin disease had left them. "We'll be able to go back to our families now," they said. "Won't it be wonderful!"

One of the ten suddenly thought of Jesus. "We ought to go back and thank Him," he said. But the others took no notice and ran off to their homes.

Only one went back to Jesus to say "Thank you." Jesus, I think, was sad that the other nine had not come back to praise God and thank Jesus.

Jesus Himself often thanked His Father. Before He fed the crowds with bread and fish, He gave thanks. He thanked God for His friends. At His Last Supper He thanked God His Father. He wants us to thank His Father too. We do this at Mass.

This
is My Beloved
Son

WE GIVE THANKS

Can you think of a time when you did something special for someone and they didn't even say "Thank you?" If so, you may remember how hurt you felt. But if someone *did* thank you, you felt good.

God our Father has been good to us. He's given us life, a beautiful world to live in, homes and parents and friends. But most especially He has given us His own dear Son, Jesus, to be our friend. And so at Mass we join Jesus in thanking and praising God our Father for all these wonderful gifts. This is why the Mass is called EUCHARIST – a Greek word which means THANKS-GIVING.

The key words to remember at this part of the Mass:

IT IS RIGHT
TO GIVE HIM THANKS AND PRAISE

Bob's Bikes
£82·00
'BMX'
DAILY NEWS

SAVING UP TO GIVE

Jimmy had a paper round. It was rather hard getting up early each morning but he was saving up for a new bike. Not an ordinary bike, you understand, but a really wonderful one, costing £82. His dad had said, "If you save up £52, I'll put the other £30 to it." This meant many weeks of paper delivering. But by November, Jimmy had saved £40.

Then one night on T.V., he saw pictures of children starving in Ethiopia. It upset him to see the thinness of the little boys and girls, with their tummies swollen, and their eyes covered with flies – they were too weak to brush the flies away.

That night when he went to bed, he found it hard to sleep. "How can I buy myself a bike," he asked himself, "when all these people are dying of hunger?"

When morning came, his mind was made up. He knew what he would do. "I'll give half of what I've saved to the children of Ethiopia," he said to himself as he dressed. "I'll just have to wait a bit longer for a bike."

His action was a big sacrifice: he was giving at a cost to himself.

JESUS'S SACRIFICE

Jesus could have run away across the River Jordan when he knew that people were coming out to arrest and kill Him. He would have been safe there in the desert where no one could have found Him. But if He had done that, He knew He would have let His Father down. Not that His Father wanted Him to die and suffer. What His Father wanted was for Jesus to teach people to love and care for and forgive each other. But many of those whom Jesus lived among and preached to didn't like what He said and so they decided to kill Him. But Jesus stood His ground. He gave His life because He knew He had to be faithful to His Father's message. He gave His life for our sake.

His death was a sacrifice because He gave all He had, His very life. At the Last Supper, Jesus had said, "Greater love no man has, than that he gives his life for his friends." That is just what Jesus Himself did.

In a very special way, that sacrifice of Jesus is made present to us at Mass.

In raising Jesus to life again on Easter Sunday, God our Father is saying to us, "Now you know that what Jesus Christ, my Son, said is true. You too must give of yourself to help others. You must join your sacrifice to His."

Can you think of something you can tell Jesus you are going to do (it may be difficult) so that Jesus will not be alone in His sacrifice?

Words to look out for in this part of the Mass:

CHRIST HAS DIED
CHRIST IS RISEN
CHRIST WILL COME AGAIN

THE CENTRE OF THE MASS

Before he was given up to death,
a death he freely accepted,
he took bread and gave you thanks.
He broke the bread,
gave it to his disciples, and said:

TAKE THIS, ALL OF YOU, AND EAT IT:

THIS IS MY BODY WHICH WILL BE GIVEN UP FOR YOU.

When supper was ended, he took the cup.
Again he gave you thanks and praise,
gave the cup to his disciples, and said:

TAKE THIS, ALL OF YOU, AND DRINK FROM IT:

THIS IS THE CUP OF MY BLOOD,
THE BLOOD OF THE NEW AND EVERLASTING CONVENANT.*
IT WILL BE SHED FOR YOU AND FOR ALL MEN
SO THAT SINS MAY BE FORGIVEN.

DO THIS IN MEMORY OF ME.

*This word *'covenant'* means an *'agreement'*, a *'promise'*, that God has made to love us always, even when we don't love Him.

MAKING FRIENDS AGAIN

Jimmy and Joey were in the same class at school and usually sat next to each other. One day when Jimmy came in after the class visit to the swimming baths he noticed something was missing from his desk. It was his wrist watch. He'd taken it off before he went because it wasn't waterproofed. Only two boys out of the whole class had not gone to the baths. Joey was one of them. He was just getting over a very bad cold and had been told not to go. Joey was indignant when Jimmy told him he was a thief. "I didn't take your watch," he said. "I've got one of my own."

Only later did Jimmy discover that the other boy was the thief. But by then Joey was so angry with Jimmy that he wouldn't speak to him even when Jimmy apologised.

But by chance the following Sunday at Mass, Jimmy and Joey were next to each other in church. The priest said: "Let us offer each other the sign of peace."

Jimmy turned to Joey and held out his hand. At first Joey tried not to see. But then smiled and the two boys shook hands.

The words to look out for at this part of the Mass are:

PEACE BE WITH YOU

HAVING A FRIEND

One of the best things about having a close friend is having someone you can talk to and someone who will listen to you when you talk. When you're feeling happy about something, or when you're sad, to have someone you can share your happiness or sadness with makes the happiness more happy and the sadness less sad when you talk about it.

When Hannah and Jimmy receive Communion at Mass, they know that it is not just bread (and wine sometimes) that people are given. What looks like bread and wine is Jesus Himself.

So when they have come back to their place in church, they sit down and quietly try and talk to Jesus; as they would to their best friend. They talk about the way they have been at home, and what they are glad or sad about, what they are a bit frightened of and lots of other things too.

The words to look out for at this part of the Mass are:

LORD, I AM NOT WORTHY

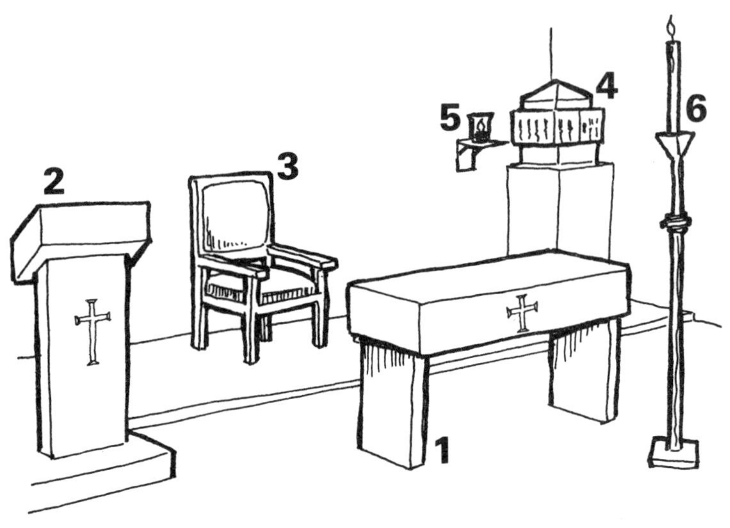

1 is the table (the altar) and reminds us of the Last Supper table.

2 is the lectern ('ambo' is another word for it) where the Bible (God's letter to us) is kept and read from.

3 is the chair, from which the priest calls us to pray.

4 is the tabernacle (a safe) where the consecrated Bread is kept.

5 is the lamp which reminds us of the Real Presence of Jesus.

6 is the Paschal (Easter) Candle, which reminds us that the resurrection means that Jesus is alive and with us now.

OTHER PRAYERS TO SAY

Think of the word A-L-T-A-R

A stands for ADORATION

Jesus, you are the Son of God.
I ADORE YOU.

L stands for LOVE

Jesus, you are my Saviour.
You gave your life for me.
I LOVE YOU.

T stands for THANKS

Jesus, thank you for being my Friend and helping me along the road back to your Father and my Father.

A stands for ASKING

Jesus, I ask you to help
my mum and dad,
my brothers and sisters,
all my relations,
all who love me and care for me
and all those too who may not care for me.
Bless them all.

R stands for RESOLVE

Jesus, I shall try to be your good friend in the week ahead.
I want to know you more clearly
follow you more nearly
and love you more dearly.

HE'S WITH US AGAIN

Hannah's elder brother, David, was taken ill very suddenly. The ambulance came and rushed him to hospital with its blue lights flashing and sirens sounding. Later that same day news came through that he had picked up a very dangerous germ. He was put into the intensive care unit.

After several days, Hannah was allowed a brief visit with her parents. David looked terribly ill and could hardly speak. He had a tube attached to his arm.

When they were out of the hospital Hannah was crying. "Is he going to die?" she asked her mum. But her mum was crying too and couldn't answer.

About a week later, the news was better. His body had managed (with a little help from doctors, nurses and medicine) to overcome the germs. He was on the road to health again.

On the night after he came home from hospital the family had a celebration. They invited the grandparents, one or two aunties and uncles, a couple of David's friends from college.

There was a great spread of food and drink. Everybody was happy.

"This is the best day of my life," said Hannah. "We thought David wasn't even going to be with us again, but he is."

It was a great celebration.

HE IS REALLY ALIVE

When Jesus was taken down from the cross, his mother, and aunt Mary and Mary Magdalen and John, his closest friend, saw just how dead Jesus was. They laid the body of Jesus on a marble shelf in the tomb cut out from rock.

All the other friends of Jesus had run away frightened, but they later met together in the upper room where they had supper together the night before Jesus died. "We've seen the last of Him," they said to one another. "I suppose I'll have to go back to fishing again," said Peter. "And I'll have to go back into that dreary tax office," said Matthew. "We had hoped He would be the one our country has waited for all these hundreds of years – the Messiah, but now all hope has gone. He is dead."

Then suddenly Jesus was there. "Peace be to you," He said. At first His friends were scared stiff. They thought He was a ghost. Jesus said, "I'm not a ghost. See, I'm really alive."

The followers of Jesus were overjoyed at Jesus being really alive, not just with the same life He'd had before, but with a new life.

"Jesus is risen from the dead," they told their friends. "He is really alive! We have seen Him."

WITH US STILL

Later, when the friends of Jesus could no longer see Him, they knew He was still with them, close to them. He had promised: "I will be with you always even to the end of the world."

When they wanted to celebrate the fact that He hadn't stayed dead but had come back to a new life, they would meet together on a Sunday (the day of the Resurrection) and they would say and do what Jesus said and did at the Last Supper (see page 37). Just like Hannah and her family celebrated the recovery from near death of her brother, David, so the parish family every Sunday celebrates together the belief that Jesus is alive and with us in our get-togethers. "Where two or three are gathered together in my name," Jesus had said, "I shall be there."

Often during Mass the priest says to us, "The Lord be with you." He is reminding us that Jesus did not go away and desert us. He has stayed with us. And on Sundays especially we meet together and are happy that our brother Jesus has won through, and wants us to share this sacred meal with Him and with one another.

THE LORD BE WITH YOU

ALLELUIA*

*'Alleluia' means 'Praise God'.

THE MASS IS ENDED

And so the Mass is ended. We have seen how:

We tell our Father we are sorry for our sins (page 13)

We listen to God's message to us (page 17)

We care for people who need help (page 23)

We thank our Father for all He has done for us (page 31)

We give ourselves in sacrifice (page 33)

We make peace with one another (page 39)

We talk with our friend Jesus (page 41)

We celebrate happily that Jesus is alive and with us (page 47)

And so now we are ready to go out and
by the way we live
by the help we give to people
we show that we are true friends of Jesus.

The words to remember at the end of Mass are:

GO IN PEACE TO LOVE AND SERVE THE LORD

THANKS BE TO GOD

POINTERS FOR PARENTS

A Different Attitude

This book is intended for that time, a couple or so years after the child has made his/her First Communion, when the glow of that first Eucharistic meeting with Jesus has begun to fade. There is a big difference in attitude between the 6–7-year-old and the 9–11-year old. The very young child is capable of a type of "contemplation", is able to wonder at the mystery of religion. The older child has usually passed beyond that stage into something much more down-to-earth and practical. She/He is interested in externals, is much more extrovert, cannot bear remaining still for long, loves to do things and become involved.

Applying these ideas to coming to Mass with your child, I don't need to tell you what difficulties await you, if the Mass is unduly prolonged, the sermon difficult, and your child has nothing to do but feel imprisoned in a pew.

In other words, my first suggestion is to find a Mass specially adapted for children. If there isn't one in your parish, could you not try to find one or two teachers, who with you, would approach the priest with an offer to help organise such a Mass. Most priests would appreciate such an approach, and if your suggestion were acted upon, could prevent a large number of 16-year-olds leaving the church through having endured ten or so years of sheer boredom.

Linking Home With Church

If you are reading this booklet, it's more than likely that you appreciate the fact that religion is much more than a "church-on-Sunday" affair. It's a round-the-clock relationship with God, through Jesus His Son, in the power of the Spirit. This means to say that the Mass is going to mean a great deal more to your child if it is somehow linked to your home life. Here are some suggestions:

Say a prayer together round the dining table before a meal. (It helps to focus attention if you have a candle.) Have some Holy Water too. It's good to have this in the home; it's not a superstition; it is a reminder of our baptism by which we were empowered to offer the Mass with the ordained priest. Make a cross on your child's forehead with it.

If there is a quarrel between the children, remind them that they will be offering each other a handshake of peace at Mass on Sunday. It would also be helpful to refer to the Liturgical seasons: Advent with an Advent wreath, Christmas with a crib, Lent with a weekly Friday "fast", Easter with a small decorated Paschal Candle, May with a Lady Altar . . . and so on. I believe that these home rituals are of greater importance in the religious development of the child than almost anything else.

Too Idealistic?

If you are beginning to think that the above suggestions are too "way out", idealistic, impractical, perhaps I could ask you to consider the likelihood of the day being not too far away when those present at Mass will only be the totally dedicated Catholics in whose homes such practices are taken for granted. Our society is becoming more and more polarised between very committed Christians and those whom one might describe as "ex-Christians". Those Catholics whose only motive for coming to Sunday Mass is to avoid sin form part of a vanishing species. Increasingly, people come because they want to, or else not at all.

Parents' Attitudes

The unspoken attitude that the parents have towards the Mass will, to a large extent, be picked up and adopted by the children. If the parents find the Mass a bore and a chore, something to be endured, almost certainly the children will look on it in the same way. Conversely, if the parents appear to value the Mass highly and look forward to the weekly outing to church, this will rub off onto the children. Even if they can't understand everything that happens at Mass, or appreciate the readings and sermon, the parents' attitude of reverence, devotion and prayerfulness will be communicated to the children. Obviously this is more difficult to achieve if the parents are of different faiths. I can suggest no easy way round this difficulty. All I would do (if I were a Catholic married to someone of another faith or none), would be to beg my spouse to offer all possible help since the future happiness of the child depends upon it.

Undoubtedly these junior years are of vital importance, and if the child is to grow up to be a practising and committed Christian, the interest and enthusiasm of both parents is indispensable.

Read Together

It would be immensely helpful if one of the parents could read this booklet (a page a night) with the child. I have tried to make it appealing to young children by using examples of everyday life. But the interest of the child would be reinforced if mum or dad were to talk about the pictures in the book and then the corresponding text. Not only would this ensure that the child understood it, but, more importantly, it would indicate in an unspoken but compelling way, just how central the Mass is to those the child loves more than anyone else.

In Church

I need hardly say that arriving early, occupying a pew from which the child can see what is happening, choosing the sort of Mass (time, type, priest-celebrant) most likely to appeal to the child, is important. Make sure that s/he brings this book along. Point out the various stages of the Mass as it proceeds. If you can offer to bring up the gifts, or read, or if your child can be invited to become a server — all these would be interesting, stimulating experiences. Keep in mind that juniors of this age dislike staying still for long. Their span of concentration is very limited unless the subject of their activity is something that interests them vitally (like football or electronic games).

Giving Thanks

The Mass was originally called 'The Breaking of Bread'. Another title was, and is, 'The Eucharist'. 'Eucharist' means giving thanks. If the Mass is to genuinely mean "Thanks be to God" for all He has done for us in Christ, then we must first have an almost non-stop attitude of gratitude to those around us. After all, why should we feel any desire to say thank you to God whom we *cannot* see, if we fail to say thank you to mum and dad, aunts and uncles, brothers and sisters, teachers and friends whom we *can* see and whose favours to us are more readily discernible. Dietrich Bonhoeffer was a Lutheran Pastor who was martyred by the Nazis in 1945. From prison he wrote to his congregation: "Only he who gives thanks for little things receives the big things." We want our children to receive the "big things" from the Mass: the joy that comes from sharing with their brothers and sisters in the parish family the worship of the living God; a share too in the life of Jesus which will carry them through to the glory of heaven. Let's make sure that at home we all show our grateful appreciation for the "little things" by affirming each other positively, by loving unselfishly, and by forgiving generously.

Anthony Bullen
St Bartholomew's
Rainhill